A Lifetime of
Adventure

A Lifetime of
Adventure

Dr. Ned Ratekin

A LIFETIME OF ADVENTURE

iUniverse books may be ordered through booksellers or by contacting:

iUniverse
1663 Liberty Drive
Bloomington, IN 47403
www.iuniverse.com
844-349-9409

ISBN: 978-1-6632-1590-1 (sc)
ISBN: 978-1-6632-1591-8 (e)

Print information available on the last page.

iUniverse rev. date: 01/08/2021

<u>Dedication</u>

For my Mother and Father
Brothers Earl, Jim Loren, and Dan
With special tribute to my wife Ruthie
And my three sons Kent, Jack, and Joel

Contents

Purpose 1

The Family 2

The Playing Years 13

Elementary School Days 20

High School Days..23

College Days 26

Here Comes The Bride..32

The Chicago Experience 35

High School Teaching 39

College Teaching...45

Our Three Sons...51

Hooked On Travel 57

The World Of B&B's...70

Troubling Times 79

Reflections 82

Ruth and Ned Ratekin

Purpose

INCREASINGLY I HAVE ASKED MYSELF how I came to realize such a favored and enjoyable life. My search always leads to the same answer, my family. First there was the family of my birth, my parents and four brothers who held me close yet let me feel free, and then my own family, my wife Ruth and three sons Kent, Jack and Joel who led the way to adventure, variety, and great joy, and then my five grandchildren and seven great-grandchildren who amaze me with their love and their enthusiasm.

Now in the ninth decade of my life, more occupied with reflecting on the past than plotting the future, I have decided I really wouldn't object to doing it all over again. But with the impossibility of that, together with a firm curiosity about my true future, I decided that I might realize the best of both worlds by recalling and sharing a few memories from the past.

The Family

A Happy Family is but an earlier heaven
                                        - George Bernard Shaw

W HEN I WAS 19 MONTHS old I had my first adventure. I
had decided to be a cowboy and asked Mom to tie a red
bandana around my neck. Then I put on an old hat and said
goodbye. Mom was busy and assumed I was just going out
in the yard. I remember I walked down Avenue A, and then
turned on 34th Street toward Broadway. I walked past the little
ice house and watched the ice truck drive by.

After a while Mom realized I had actually left and went
outside to find me gone. She was looking up and down streets
when the ice truck stopped, and the driver asked her if she
was looking for a little boy. He told her to get in and he would
take her to him. They found me playing with an older man
who was determined I shouldn't get to busy Broadway. In my
fifth-grade autobiography I wrote: "Then the ice man was kind
enough to give us a ride all the way back home." Little did I
know then how many more adventures I would safely enjoy in
my fortunate life.

It all started in Council Bluffs, Iowa. We were five boys,
Earl, Jim, Ned, Loren, and Dan, blessed with a Mom (Dorothy)
and Dad (Harry) who did not let the Great Depression overcome
their task of building a solid family. Mom was always busy,
keeping clothes clean, ironed and mended, providing breakfasts,
school lunches, and solid evening meals, and teaching us how
to do all that, keeping order and health in the home, and talking
and teaching about what was happening in the neighborhood
and in the nation.

Mom knew everything, of course, so when I pondered over

a piece of coal I found on the ground by our basement coal chute, I went to Mom in the kitchen, held up my black nugget, and asked "Where does coal come from?" Mom explained that coal comes from things like wood that have been in the ground a long time. As a four-year-old with a limited concept of "a long time" I decided to make some coal. I found a small piece of wood from an orange crate, dug a hole at least four or five inches deep in the back yard, planted the "wood", tamped down the dirt, and waited all day and all night — a long time.

The next morning, I ran out to dig up my coal – to find no change except smudges of dirt on the wood. I showed Mom my stubborn piece of wood for an explanation. She laughed, gave me a hug, and explained that the coal we have today was wood a long, long time ago, even before I was born. Years later I read about the layer of plants that became coal existed about 3 million years ago, and I realized Mom was always a dependable source.

Dad's formal schooling ended early, but with personal effort he had developed accounting and business skills through self-study, a local business school, and later at the University of Omaha. Early in the marriage, Dad's career plans received a major blow. The new millwork business he was creating with two partners was lost, a victim of the Depression. Dad scrambled. He always found work, sometimes hitchhiking for miles. He went on to develop a successful tax accounting and business career, even serving as President of the Iowa Bookkeepers Association.

Despite his struggles in those lean years, Dad always had his family in mind. One day when I was about five years old, Mom told us that Dad was working in the basement, and we could not go down there. I was a little puzzled, but on Christmas morning I found out why. Dad had retrieved the runners from some old, discarded sleds and in the basement rebuilt them into brand new, freshly painted sleds. That Christmas present gave us many years of happy sledding.

By the time Earl, born in 1925, was 10 years old he had become a trusted aide to Mom in maintaining the household, earning the role of being in charge of his younger siblings when Mom had errands to run or a friend in need of a visit. On one occasion, when Mom was away on an errand, Earl discovered a dime while examining the contents of a bureau drawer. He excitedly told his charges that we were going on a trip to the store, just a block away across the streetcar tracks. He made sure we were properly dressed in jackets and hats, and then led us to the corner grocery which had a special counter where you could buy an ice cream cone. He spent his dime on a vanilla cone, and we stood there, passing the cone around for a lick or a bite until it was gone.

I remember being impressed with Earl's ability to plan and carry out such a major adventure. Earl cared for us, joined the Navy, saw real battle in the South Pacific, married wisely, became a corporate accountant, cared for a family of two sons and two daughters, and then, because all four of his brothers had established homes elsewhere, he willingly and carefully cared for Mom and Dad in their later years.

I always thought that Jim, born in 1926 and squeezed in between Earl and me, found justice in a life of adventure and daring. In the subsiding years of World War II Jim joined the army, eventually serving General Douglas MacArthur in his Headquarters in the Dai-Ichi building in Tokyo. Also, as a member of the Army Reserve Jim was called back to serve in the Korean War, where, perhaps due to his B.A. in Psychology from the University of Omaha, he was assigned to the daunting role of counseling young men returning from battle.

Jim was attracted to the employment possibilities of California and moved with wife Genevieve to the Los Angeles area. There he successfully grew his business career and, with Genevieve, a well-balanced family by number and careers, of two boys and two girls. At a family reunion recently, Jim revealed his style of decision-making that had served him well, and he commended it to other Ratekins, young or old. He explained that he found little interest in applying for a task, a job, or a career for which he was already qualified. Rather, he was attracted to challenging tasks that would provide discovery of new abilities, adventure, and heightened rewards. He admitted that not everyone might understand such bold evidence of confidence, but he persevered and succeeded, eventually retiring from a major business career, greatly respected for his national and international service.

Loren, born in 1933, completed a B.A. degree at Parsons College and an M.A. degree at the University of Iowa. Loren was an educator and wife Betty was an attorney in Burlington. Loren taught business and history courses and became a school administrator. He was a true historian, punctuating enjoyable discussions with the phrase "Did you know that—" followed by intriguing observations on Iowa Native Americans or presidential behavior. Many of his accounts were documentations of why I should be proud to be an Iowan.

Loren was also a sportsman, playing high school football until he was injured, and then becoming skillful in the more enduring sports of tennis and golf. In his later years Loren stepped out on the stage, appearing in productions of Burlington, Iowa's Community Theatre. Loren's greatest contest was his battle with cancer. He endured several challenges, surviving with family care and medical skill until succumbing at the age of 84.

Dan, born in 1936, became a school counselor, well equipped to observe and advise with his Parsons B.A. and Iowa M.A. It was a match so expected to endure, that when he and wife Betty (We discriminated by the terms "Loren's Betty" or "Dan's Betty") announced they were opening a restaurant in Des Moines we were surprised, but we admired their confidence and courage. With just the right menus and services they created a unique offering for office workers in downtown Des Moines. Success led to expansion to three locations, one on the Des Moines' skywalk, and finally to a location within the new 44 story 801 Grand building, the tallest building in Iowa.

"Fondness" is the best term I can come up with to characterize relations among the five of us as brothers. We were not constant in recognizing birthdays, and we were pressed to name all our nieces, nephews, especially their grandchildren. But we were always happy to see each other when events brought us together, were honestly concerned about each other's welfare, and often laughed together over shared events, especially those we thought were unknown to Mom and Dad.

DAD'S FAMILY

The population of the American Colonies rose rapidly after 1700 when a flood of over 400,000 Scots-Irish immigrants, many from the Ulster region of Ireland, arrived seeking escape from poverty and religious intolerance. "Scots-Irish" refers to the ethnic group centered in Ulster County in Ireland, largely populated by descendants of previous immigrants from the lowlands of Scotland. Evidently, the reason for that previous migration was again, escape from poverty and religious intolerance.

Shortly after 1750, four brothers, Lawrence, James, Patrick, and John Ratekin were among those Scots-Irish immigrants seeking a livelihood in the English colonies. The specific year of their arrival is not known, but some approximation may be found in the dates of their deaths: Lawrence, before 1785; James, 1813; Patrick, 1804; and John, approximately 1800. Those dates indicate that they were in the colonies during the period of the American Revolution. Also, the specific location of their early settlement in the colonies is not known, although there are references to Pennsylvania and Virginia. Over the centuries since the arrival of the four Ratekin brothers several variations of the family name occurred among the male descendants. According to the results of extensive research provided by Cousin Bruce Ratekin of Ohio, those name variations include: Ratekin, Rattekin, Rattican, Rattikin, Radican, and Radekin.

During the time when the Ratekins arrived in America, the increasing population of the coastal colonies reduced the availability of farm land for new arrivals, and the Appalachian Mountains formed a serious barrier to travel to the fertile lands to the west. In 1775 the Transylvania Land Company hired Daniel Boone to create a trail through the Cumberland Gap to help new arrivals gain access to the valuable land beyond.

The Ratekin brothers joined this pursuit of productive land. Every distant Ratekin relative I have met has repeated the story of the role Daniel Boone played in the family's travels west. They all have been told that Boone blazed their trail and guided them through hidden passes, around peaks, and past unfriendly Native Americans to arrive in the rich lands now known as Kentucky and Tennessee. Whether any Ratekins actually met Daniel Boone is unknown, but it is known that Boone played a major role in that westward movement. It has been estimated that the trail, known as the Wilderness Road, became a route for over 300,000 settlers to <u>gain access to the fertile land in Kentucky,</u> Tennessee, and many points west.

The family of my Dad's father, Clyde Ratekin, moved westward with the many other Scots-Irish of the time, living in Illinois, Missouri, southwest Iowa, and eventually to Omaha, Nebraska. My Dad was born in Omaha and later moved with family to the West End of Council Bluffs. Council Bluffs was the terminus of the eastern route of the Union Pacific Railroad and the connection with the western route. Grandfather Clyde was a scheduler for Union Pacific and Dad sometimes traveled with his father to Denver on railroad business. In 1930 Clyde died on one of these trips by himself, and Dad had to travel to Colorado to bring his body back to Council Bluffs.

Our family descends from John Ratekin, the youngest of the Scots-Irish brothers arriving in America in the late 1700's. Birth and death dates of John's descendants in direct male line within my family are:

John Ratekin	? - 1780 ?
John Ratekin Jr.	? - 1831
Joseph Sylvester Ratekin	1785 - 1867
George Washington Ratekin	1820 - 1912
Clyde Provin Ratekin	1871 - 1930
Harry Earl Ratekin	1902 - 1995
m. Dorothy Lois Grason	1903 - 2004
Earl Grason Ratekin	1925 - 2020
James Alvin Ratekin	1926 -
Ned Harry Ratekin	1929 -
m. Ruth Elaine Odean	1927 - 2017
Kent O'Dean Ratekin	1953 –
Jack Grason Ratekin	1957 - 2018

Joel Carlson Ratekin   1961-
Loren Dale Ratekin   1933-2017
Daniel Lee Ratekin   1936 -

MOM'S FAMILY

On January 2, 1777, Mrs. Joseph Sayre sat in her door yard in Trenton, New Jersey, writing a letter to her husband, a member of the revolutionary army under General George Washington. She writes that she can hear the cannon from the battle he is fighting against the British, and she is praying that he will return home safely. The battle she hears is known as the Second Battle of Trenton, or the Battle of the Assunpink. Mrs. Sayre was the great, great, grandmother of Dorothy Lois Grason, my mother. That letter in delightful handwriting has been saved and handed down in the family over generations.

Mom's mother, Lenora Sayre, was English. Mom often described the care her mother would take in preparing and serving "tea". Mom was proud of her family's claim to a significant artist in its lineage. Fred Grayson Sayre, born in Medoc Missouri in 1879, first achieved considerable status as a commercial artist in St. Louis and Omaha, Nebraska. In 1915, when his life was threatened by an extreme case of diphtheria, his doctor recommended that he move to the southwest desert as the only possible means of survival. He was fascinated by the desert landscape and became one of California's most popular desert artists. Copies of his paintings may still be found in art stores and tourist shops. A main body of his works has been acquired by the Redfern Gallery in Laguna Beach, California. Fred Grayson Sayre died in 1939.

My mother's father, Jacob Grason, was also English, with

family migrating to Canada, and later to Wisconsin in the United States. Jacob was born in Monroe Wisconsin on May 9, 1857 and moved with his parents to Jasper County, Missouri in 1866. Jacob attended high school at Carthage, Missouri and majored in business and education at Park College in Parkville, Missouri.

Jacob learned the milling trade from his father and worked with him briefly and then began teaching. He developed a method of shorthand that became widely used. As a result, he became employed as a teacher in the Council Bluffs High School to teach his shorthand method and other business courses. Eventually he became Head of the school's Commercial Department. Jacob was elected as a representative to the Iowa Legislature in Des Moines in 1914, where he became a major contributor to legislation establishing the Iowa Public Employees Retirement System (IPERS). Jacob and Lenora were married on June 23. 1880, in Medoc Missouri and had seven children. A younger one of those was Dorothy, my mother.

A MOVE TO THE HIGHLANDS

A glance at a Council Bluffs street map will reveal a significant aspect of the city. In the West half, from the Missouri River toward the historical center of the city, the streets are well ordered in tidy blocks of parallel streets and avenues. These are the streets and avenues that fall in the flat area of the river valley, locally known as the West End. The Streets in the east half of the city appear to be randomly drawn curved lines, starting and ending in no special design. These constitute the streets of the city that weave through the loess hills, the phenomenon formed over eons by dust-borne winds from the west.

I was born and lived for six years in the West End. One day Mom said, "We're moving to the hills. Ever since we've lived in the West End someone has been sick, or we've had problems of one kind or another." I knew Mom was right about being sick. In a few short years I had measles, mumps, chicken pox, and scarlet fever. Brother Loren stepped in a pan of boiling hot water. Our house and all those in it were quarantined, and Dad had to live in the garage for a while so he could go to work. So, we moved to the hills, to a house on a street and to schools that had names instead of numbers - Pierce, Madison, and Bloomer - and we had much more fun with our sleds in the hills.

Mom and Dad
Dorothy and Harry Ratekin

**Dan, Loren, Ned, Earl, and Jim
with Mom in front of her grandfather clock
birthday gift to Risen Son Village**

The Playing Years

Summer will end soon enough, and childhood as well.

- George R.R. Martin

S CHOOL WAS CENTRAL IN MY childhood years, of course, but long days, weekends, and summers gave time for many other adventures. We lived in the city, but our houses were in areas with much open ground, nearby fields, and deep woods. So, we played ball in the fields, played Indians in the woods, dug caves in the clay hillsides, had carnivals in the open lots, skied down hills on barrel staves, and played hockey on Mosquito creek on ice-skates that were clamped on our shoes, just like roller skates were at that time.

Most of the fun we had in those early years was make-shift. Constantly rummaging in cast-off junk piles and waste-bins, we made scooters out of old roller skates and peach boxes, go-carts from orange crates and wheels from abandoned wagons, and rubber guns from crate ends and worn-out inner tubes. We were outside — climbing, chasing, deciding what to build next from our assortment of collected cast-offs, and exploring the woods, convinced we were direct descendants of the original Pottawatomies in those loess hills.

I must have been 9 or 10 years old when I was reading about how Indians made their houses in the woods. According to that account they would find a group of well rooted saplings, pick out a few in a circle, bend those over and tie them together at the top, clear out the growth under them, use the cuttings to weave walls between saplings, and move in. I wondered if I could do that, so I tried, and it really worked just like the book said. A few days later Mom asked me why I was taking some food and other things into the woods, so I told Mom about my Indian hut. Now I never, ever, saw Mom go into the woods, so I was surprised when she told me a few days later that she had found my hut, and thought it was nice. I was surprised because taking care of a household with five kids left her little time to go walking in the woods. I also was pleased. I thought maybe she was checking on what I was really doing in the woods and came away satisfied.

I made a crystal set out of cast-off parts of radios and tin cans. I used the cardboard tube from a roll of toilet paper as a base for the coil. (Toilet paper tubes were firmer then.) I wrapped the tube with wire from the scrapyard after stripping off all the insulation. I cut a tuner arm from a tin can and used a piece of firm wire for the crystal scanner. The old set of earphones still worked. I would go to bed and listen to The Green Hornet, The Lone Ranger, and Roy Rogers until Mom would come by and tell me to go to sleep.

My next-door neighbor and school mate Ralph liked to build things too. One day he suggested that we rig up a telephone between our houses. We read about how to do that, and then with about 30 feet of wire strung out my bedroom window into his, old telephone parts from the scrap yard, and a transformer from a train set, we were ready to make our trial call. He ran home and started talking, but it wasn't working. So, he came back over to my house to help identify the problem. We had our heads together examining my wiring when clear as a bell Ralph's mother's voice came over our telephone: "Ralph, are you over there?" Surely as exciting as Alexander Graham Bell's: "Mr. Watson – Come here – I want to see you".

I don't recall the specific sea-faring story that got me started, maybe *Two Years Before the Mast*, or one of the Nordoff and Hall series, but I became interested in sailing ships. I probably would have never known the firm meaning of capstan, fo'castle, rigging, fore and aft, port and starboard, without my fascination for those stories. I was especially impressed by the three-masted ship, like the Cutty Sark. I carved a few ships, even added cloth sails. I remember boring Mom with my nautical knowledge by pointing out all the parts of one of my clipper ships.

Also, I remember having lots of fun shooting marbles with my friends — little-circle marbles, big-circle marbles, and pots. The game of pots was my favorite. I still have a small can of marbles with a couple of boulders. I don't know why people don't shoot marbles anymore.

School is the place you go to learn, as in "What school do you attend? School is what happens there, as in "Do you like school? And school is where you find identity, as in "My school is better than your school." In elementary school we organized for football by school, with no reference to whether we liked school, and with no approval, support, or equipment from the school. So, our team was Madison, and our greatest fear was playing Washington, the team with kids from the large elementary school downtown. The season schedule was loosely organized through contacts with cousins or friends from the other schools. There were no adults involved. A couple players on our team did have helmets and shoulder pads provided by fearful parents. In seventh grade we finally beat Washington, but we weren't expecting it when a rag-tag team from Gunn School beat us that year. We thought maybe they had more players with shoulder pads, but we realized our problem was we had the game won before we played.

CHORES

But it wasn't all play and fun. We had chores, too. With a coal fired furnace you need to put coal in and take ashes out. After cooling in a metal bucket, the ashes were usually spread on the clay road running up the hill by our house. There was setting the table for seven, peeling potatoes and watching them cook, washing and drying the dishes, lighting the water heater and filling the wash tubs, hanging out the wash, taking in the wash, helping with the ironing, sweeping the floors, dusting the furniture, mowing the grass with a rotary push mower, mending socks, half soling shoes, shoveling snow, watching little brothers, feeding the little brother, emptying ice box water, fixing the bicycle, dressing for church. Since all five of us were boys, there were no gender specific tasks, and I have always been thankful for the small advantage I had over some of my male friends when it came to kitchen and clothes-care tasks.

POCKET MONEY

Intermittently we would ask Mom and Dad about the possibility of an allowance. The answer was never "No", only a "We'll see." I soon saw that the decision was unlikely to come into focus, so my search for other means of gaining capital began early. I remember when I was about ten years old carrying a market basket and a garden trowel around to my neighbors, offering to dig up their dandelions-for a fee. After a few efforts I gained a customer and spent a substantial time digging up yellow dandelions and putting them in my basket. She gave me a dime, and I thought "success", and proceeded to knock on another door.

The lady of the house opened the door, and I began my

pitch on solving her dandelion problem. She looked at my basket of harvested dandelions and said "Dandelions! I don't need any more dandelions—look at my yard—I already have plenty of dandelions!" and before I could appeal, she quickly closed the door. Years later that experience was repeated when I tried to sell tableware door to door. My net sales record was one sale. I realized that sales should not be high on my list of potential careers.

I cannot recall a time from age 12 to decades later, when we closed the doors on The Carlson House Bed and Breakfast in 2002, that I was not involved in some form of working to gain a few extra dollars. That was due, I was led to believe, because of my Sottish ancestry. I was 12 years old when the owner of the corner grocery across the street from our house asked me if I wanted to help in his store. My primary duties were to stock shelves and keep the floor swept and tidy. He soon relied on me to check out customers when he was busy filling orders behind the meat counter. To help me in that role he first taught me how to make change. I didn't realize at the time that he was giving me a skill that served me well over many years of sales and clerking.

We did not have sacks for customers' purchases, just a wide roll of brown paper with an attached paper cutter at the end of the counter and string hanging down from a spool near the ceiling. The process was to guess how much paper to tear off, wrap and tie the purchase, and then cut off the string.

With that experience I was able to apply successfully for an after school and week-end job stocking shelves and checking out customers at Herschel's Wigwam Grocery at First Street and Broadway downtown. I was successful in the job with one significant failure. It occurred while making change. It was my first encounter with intentional theft, and I couldn't believe how dumb I was. A customer with a suitcase bought a five-cent pack of gum and handed me a dollar. I gave him the change which he placed on the counter, saying "Altogether I think I have two dollars in change here," pulling a handful of coins from his pocket. "It would be handy if you would give me two dollar bills for it." I counted the $2 in change on the counter and promptly handed him two one-dollar bills which he placed on the counter on top of the change. Then he discovered another dollar bill in his pocket, placed it on the $4 pile of change and bills on the counter, and said, "Just give me a five-dollar bill for all of this." I did. Two seconds after the door closed, I realized my error and ran to the door. He had disappeared already. Herschel was merciful and told me to chalk it up to experience. He didn't charge me for the $2 loss, and I learned a new lesson in making change.

Finding Work around school hours, weekends and summers was almost universal among my age-mates, providing a flow of information about where jobs could be found or avoided. Some of the jobs I held during my adolescent years included stocking shelves at a Wonderbread bakery outlet, working as a soda jerk at Walgreens Drugstore, delivering the Lady's Home Journal and Saturday Evening Post to subscribers, constructing and installing truck racks for Omaha Standard Truck Company, working as a "gandy dancer" or section hand on the Wabash Railroad, and on the bridge building crew for the CB&Q Railroad.

One job brought me awareness of current national legislation. Dad, an accountant for Dwarfies Cereal Company, suggested that I apply for an open job at his company known for its popped wheat and popped rice breakfast cereal. I was employed and worked on the assembly line for several weeks packing cereal for shipment. Dad came home from work one evening and said we needed to talk. I hoped nothing was wrong with my work performance. It was decided, he said, that my job fell under the recently passed Fair Labor Standards Act which required a person to be 16 years old for that position. I was one year short.

Elementary School Days

School is a building which has four walls with tomorrow inside.

—Lon Watters

I WAS BORN IN NOVEMBER 1929 two months late for the deadline to enter kindergarten in 1934. Therefore, In January I joined the small group of children who were placed in classes as mid-year students. When many of my playground friends were in grade 2-1, I was in grade 1-2. When I was in grade 6-1, I completed that grade and grade 6-2 simultaneously, finally becoming no longer the oldest in my class but among the youngest. I believe my additional aging before entering school was to my advantage.

From kindergarten through grade eight I attended three elementary schools, Avenue B School, Pierce School, and Madison School. I attended Bloomer Junior High School for grade 9, and then Abraham Lincoln High School for grades 10 through 12.

Some people titter when I mention Bloomer School due to their benighted view of bloomers as a reference to women's underthings. Amelia Bloomer, an early suffragist and social activist from Council Bluffs for whom the school was named advocated that women wear the baggy knee-length trousers instead of long skirts to allow them more freedom and skill in athletic activities. Conservative troublemakers responded with such posters as "Amelia, you forgot your skirt!" The fact is that bloomers became quite stylish and were worn with shortened skirts.

I enjoyed school and progressed with average performance. My greatest interest was in recess and lunch time — until fifth grade. In fifth grade we began a study of world history, with a text book filled with pictures and accounts of events in places like Europe and Africa. There was a picture of the Matterhorn, a mountain in the Alps with one side in Switzerland and the other in Italy, and a picture of soldiers on horseback with red uniforms and tall hats guarding the King of England. I thought things like that would be worth seeing.

By the eighth grade in history class we were studying about the lives of people in foreign countries like England, Ireland, Scotland, and Sweden, and why so many people from those countries moved to America. Our teacher was Miss Jasper. Miss Jasper was not only our teacher, but also the school principal, so she often needed to leave class for a while. That was no problem. She was creative in making sure our learning continued even when she wasn't there, with readings and projects in her assignments.

One of these assignments was to write a story or make a diorama of what life was like in one of the countries we were studying to show why so many people came to America. I was reading about life for workers in England, so I decided to make a diorama of a lord's manor house, and his serfs working in the fields. With colored clay for people and animals, sticks for structures, and grass for the fields, I made my display. The time came for Miss Jasper to ask me to explain my project to the class. I carefully pointed out the lord's manor house and the "pheasants" working in the fields. Miss Jasper complimented me on the project, and then quietly informed me that she thought those people working in the fields are called "peasants", not "pheasants". I never went pheasant hunting without recalling Miss Jasper's kind correction.

I was a bit above average in size during my early adolescent years. Dick Eckert was the only classmate taller than me. With that advantage I was active and somewhat successful in ninth grade athletics at Bloomer School. At the year-end honor assembly, I thought some recognition might come my way, but honors in football, basketball, and track came and went without a mention of my name. I was chastising myself for such unrealistic hopes when the speaker said there was one more honor, the Scholar-Athlete Award. I was dumfounded when I heard my name, and I decided that to be called a scholar took away some of the pain from my wounded athlete ego.

High School Days

Don't Let Yourself forget what it's like to be sixteen.

- Anonymous

TODAY, HIGH SCHOOLS PROVIDE STUDENTS a variety of goal choices based on specific careers and areas of personal performance. When I entered Abraham Lincoln High School I was asked to pick one of only two choices (1) an emphasis on preparation for college studies, or (2) general education for immediate employment. I was unsure, but college preparation seemed to leave the most doors open, and Mom and Dad agreed. As the future unraveled, I was thankful for that choice. The additional requirements in language, math and sciences were a great help in my later studies, and I became especially aware of the value of the required two semesters of Latin.

My academic performance in high school across all studies was not outstanding. Nevertheless, I was somehow attracted to the precision of language study and the romance and escape of literature. That interest led to my selection of language and literature as the major areas of my later continuing studies. Some may wonder why I would choose the tedium of language studies and pondering over how to out-guess the teacher concerning "What is the author actually saying?" could hold much interest. I have one answer to that - my teachers. I came to realize the strength of my Council Bluffs public schooling as I compared it with the performance of fellow students from other Iowa schools and beyond. I have no problem remembering the name of my 12th grade English teacher - Grace Taylor. Miss Taylor was older, nearing retirement, but not past her prime. She knew literature, and she knew adolescents.

HIGH SCHOOL ATHLETICS

I participated in the sport of the season throughout my high school years. Although I was awarded athletic letters yearly in Football, Basketball, and Track and Field, my proficiency varied considerably. I was least proficient in basketball. I understood the point of the game was to put the ball in the basket, so whenever I acquired the ball, I would throw it toward the basket, often unsuccessfully. I was slow in gaining the concepts of screening, passing to gain an open good shooter, and then passing him the ball. Therefore, I spent much of my time on the bench, admiring the skill of good players like Bill Strachan, who knew how to work himself open and make a basket almost every time. In Track and Field events my running was primarily in short distance speed races and relays.

The area in which I made the most contribution to the track team was in the weight events, the discus-throw and shot-put. Football was my favorite sport. In those days, the roster of players on the field rarely changed in a change from offensive to defensive play. I was a lineman and usually on the starting roster, so I had the good fortune of being able to play a lot of football. I really enjoyed that. If anyone wonders if players really can hear cheers from the stands, the answer is "yes", and they do make a difference.

RESERVE OFFICERS TRAINING CORP

With rare exceptions, all male students in Council Bluffs high schools were required to participate in military training in the ROTC program. With the real presence of war at the time, there was a serious climate about that training including required uniforms, marching, field maneuvers, and firearm training. A

U.S. Army officer directed the program. The group at AL High School was classified as a regiment, with ranks of cadet officers mirroring positions in the US Army. Over the years I served in the progress of ranks from squad leader, Company Commander, Plans and Training Officer, Lieutenant Colonel of the Regiment, to a final promotion to Colonel of the Regiment. That last promotion was primarily a token, revealed at a spring school dance named "The Military Ball" in the waning days of my senior year and complete with the simultaneous announcement of the Honorary Colonel of the Regiment, Norma Olsen.

MAKING MUSIC

With my classes, athletic, and ROTC activities, part time jobs and chores at home I now wonder how I decided to take the time to be also in the school music program. I believe that I must have attacked some of those duties with limited rigor. I did sing in the high school choir, a madrigal group, a boy's quartet, and in school musical productions, playing the role of Samuel in Gilbert and Sullivan's *Pirates of Penzance*.

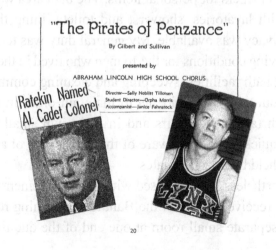

"The Pirates of Penzance"
By Gilbert and Sullivan

presented by

ABRAHAM LINCOLN HIGH SCHOOL CHORUS

Director—Sally Noblitt Tillotsen
Student Director—Orpha Morris
Accompanist—Janice Fahnstock

Ratekin Named AL Cadet Colonel

20

College Days

It is, sir, a small college, but there are those who love it.

- Daniel Webster

R OY LAWSON, MY HIGH SCHOOL football coach and a graduate of Parsons College in Fairfield, Iowa, hinted that Parsons might be a good fit for me. Also, Parsons was associated with the Presbyterian Church, which was attractive to Mom and Dad who would be helping me with finances. Parsons accepted my application, and in the fall of 1947, I traveled by train to Fairfield. I did not realize then that I would never again, except for visits, be living at home in Council Bluffs, Iowa.

During my first year at Parsons Mom and Dad paid the tuition of $150 each semester. The costs of board and room were my responsibility. Fortunately, I gained the position of "manager" (actually custodian) of one of the new quonset huts built to meet the post-war exploding demand for student housing. The residents of the "dorm" had bunk beds lining the walls and lockers for personal items. The bath area was a large space with lavatories, showers, and toilets lining the walls. Little privacy was available. My general duty was to maintain decent living conditions for the 16 men who lived in the "dorm", cleaning bath facilities, sweeping and cleaning common areas and encouraging the residents to maintain order in the open area with tables and chairs and in their own small personal areas. I quickly became aware of the wide range of a sense of "order" held by my classmates.

Nevertheless, I was pleased with the arrangements. For my efforts I received meals in the Ballard Hall dining room, and I had a separate small room at one end of the quonset with a bed, a real closet, and windows. For the ready cash I needed for personal expenses I had two sources. The business office of the college kept an "employment" list of Fairfield residents who requested help from college students for typical home tasks, like changing screens and storm windows and mowing lawns. Also, I worked for the campus crew. With all the buildings, lawns, fields, construction, and repairs, there was no end of work possible with that crew.

Many traditions characterized life on small college campuses when I entered college, and Parsons was no exception. The school's colors were green and rose, and freshmen were notified that they must always wear their green and pink beanies on campus or suffer certain consequences, like kneeling before the upper classman making the charge and singing the alma mater. In 1947 men and women returning from the battlefield were flooding college campuses, recovering their interrupted lives and taking advantage of the G.I. Bill, which provided college education expenses. Many of these veterans were freshmen, and it should be no surprise how they viewed that beanie "silliness". Freshmen wearing beanies became one of the college traditions that rapidly disappeared at Parsons College and at many colleges in the nation.

At Parsons I followed the typical liberal arts programs of courses: history, English, science, and math. My greatest struggles were with advanced mathematics and my high anxiety over the required speech course. My plans then included eventually entering the ministry, and I organized my studies accordingly. When we lived in the West End of Council Bluffs, I was baptized in Dodge Memorial Congregational Church. When we moved into hill country the family joined Grace Presbyterian Church. Mom and Dad were committed church members, regularly serving on church boards and teaching.

Dad even became a lay minister for the small Presbyterian church at Lake Manawa.

I closely followed their commitment and gladly joined them, serving often as an officer in our church youth group, singing in the choir, and joining in church activities. Eventually I became treasurer of Westminster Fellowship, a national organization of Presbyterian high school and college youth. During my Freshman year at Parsons I attended the national conference of the organization at Hanover College in Indiana.

I followed the liberal arts degree program with an emphasis in English and a few additional courses in bible and religion. During my Junior year I served as Youth Director for the Fairfield Methodist church, and as a senior I provided "pulpit supply" for small congregations near Fairfield. My remuneration often came straight from the collection plates.

I enjoyed college life: pinochle in the student union until class time, Saturday night dances at the local armory, TKE fraternity parties with the Empyrean Sorority, and attempting to generate success for our athletic teams from the stands. Also, I remain pleased with the quality of instruction I experienced. Older, dedicated faculty like George Suderman in History and Winifred Watts in literature really made the place feel like "Halls of Ivy", and the effort of younger faculty with newer degrees proving their scholarship made classes worthwhile.

My most impressive college experience was meeting and getting to know Ruth O'Dean. Ruthie was in her senior year, completing a B.A. degree in Economics and a final year of French when I arrived at Parsons College as a freshman. I first met her over registration details in the college business office where she worked. And then, there she was again as I was buying texts in the college book store which she managed. Parsons College required attendance at a weekly chapel service, as was true at many church related colleges. When I attended my first Chapel service the person standing at the door collecting attendance slips was Ruth O'Dean. I thought I would smile this time, and she smiled back. By the way, that requirement for chapel attendance eventually went the way of the green and pink beanies.

I had decided to try out for the Parsons football team, and after some success I called Mom to tell her I would be playing football. "I don't think so," she replied. "If you have time to do something like that, you should sing in the choir." By that time Mom had started to send me a check for $5 each month. I decided not to jeopardize that flow of funds, so I resigned from football and joined the choir. It was while in the choir that I became friends with Ruth O'Dean. We even sang and danced together in a production of *South Pacific*. I always thanked Mom for her objection to my plans.

By tradition, at Parsons each class level selected officers who served to organize student activities. Ruthie was president of the senior class, and I became president of the freshman class at a class meeting. So, again I was interacting with Ruth O'Dean. By springtime, Ruthie and I had a couple of dates. I recall one instance when Ruthie and I, together with good friend Bill Reed and his eventual wife Wanda, traveled in Bill's car to Burlington for a concert by Stan Kenton and his orchestra.

Then it became time for Ruthie to graduate, and I became concerned. Ruth graduated with a B.A. in Economics with cum laude and Phi Kappa Phi academic honors. I was sure she would soon become employed and find a career or a close friend elsewhere. After all, she did have other good friends. In fact, several of Ruthie's friends, especially males, called Ruthie "Rosie", assuming an Irish heritage from O'Dean, as in Rosie O'Grady. Ruthie did become employed, but to my good fortune, she was employed by Parsons College as Assistant Financial Manager.

My brother Loren joined me as at Parsons College in 1950, and brother Dan arrived on campus three years later in 1953. Not only did all three of us graduate from Parsons, but all three of us also met fellow students (coeds) who became our wives. Loren married Betty Droe, and Dan married Betty Freeman.

The Rejected Beanie

Here Comes The Bride

*My most brilliant achievement was my ability to
be able to persuade my wife to marry me.*
— Winston Churchill

B Y THE END OF MY junior year at Parsons I had been dating
Ruthie for two years. We had become pretty firm in our
relationship. Ruthie had visited my family in Council Bluffs,
and I had attended many meals, picnics, and holidays with
Ruth's parents and the families of her two married sisters,
Lucille and Mahlon Aronson and Margaret and Dale Swenson
and their children. I even had gone fishing with her father
Fred and many times had praised her mother Minnie for her
delicious Swedish meals.

I was 20 years old when I told Mom and Dad that I was
planning to propose marriage to Ruthie. They were uneasy and
suggested that I was a bit young for marriage, also noting that I
had more schooling in the future. Ruthie was 23, and my view
was that the average wasn't that far out of line. I understood
their concern and appreciated their eventual approval. In fact,
Mom helped me with decisions about the engagement ring.
Fortunately, during a visit to Council Bluffs, Ruthie said "Yes",
and we set the date for June 4, 1950.

I attended First Presbyterian Church in Fairfield, and
recently Ruthie had been attending with me. She decided that
First Presbyterian would be the best church for the wedding.
We were married by Dr. Curtis Douglas, church pastor. Ruthie's
Matron of honor was her longtime friend Margaret (Hinkhouse)
Killian who had recently married Frank Killian, a classmate
from New Jersey and one of those returning servicemen. Her
Bride's Maids were friends Martha Calhoun, who later married

Cal Solem, another returning serviceman and one of Ruthie's long-time friends, and another close friend Marilyn (Twink) Starr, who eventually married Roxie Ball. The flower girl was Linda Swenson, four-year-old daughter of Ruthie's sister Margaret (Peg). My brother Earl was Best Man, Jim, Loren, and Dan ushered and lit candles. Friend Doug McConnaha sang "O Perfect Love" and another favorite wedding song. The whole ceremony was meaningful, and Ruthie was beautiful.

Following the reception, the plan was for Cal Solem and Martha Calhoun to drive us to the hotel in Ottumwa, where Mom and Dad would pick us up the next morning, drive us back to their home in Council Bluffs, and loan us their car for a few days of Honeymoon at Spirit Lake in northwest Iowa. Margaret and Frank Killian came with us on the trip to Ottumwa. Cal drove us as he promised, but with a few variations. He told us he knew things had been hectic, so he thought we deserved a slow, restful ride to Ottumwa, away from the busy highway. He took every small county road, paved or not, for the 20-mile trip. Before we got to the hotel, he stopped at a popular night club outside of Ottumwa. "You can't have a wedding without dancing," he said, and he herded us all inside, and we danced. It was wonderful.

We moved our few belongings into a small furnished home rented from Spanish Professor W. Jefferson Dennis and located just outside the Parsons' campus gates. I added a dressing table for Ruthie made of orange crates, with a cloth skirt around it. Although I worked on campus, preached on several Sundays, and had various odd jobs, Ruthie maintained us with her employment in the Business Office of the College. We felt good together. I had been approved for admission to McCormick Theological Seminary of the Presbyterian Church (USA) located in Chicago, Ruthie was supportive of my (our) plan for me to continue studies there, and I had to make sure that I successfully completed all degree requirements for my B.A. in English at Parsons. Therefore, I was a bit more assiduous in attending class and studying than previously. I frequently studied with friend Bill Reed, who took many of the same courses as I did and had a novel and demanding method of studying and preparing for tests that served me well.

Now we needed some means of transportation. Fortunately, my TKE Fraternity brother Jim Portman of Fairfield was giving up on his 1936 Plymouth coupe, which had smooth tires, a few dents, and a driver's door that would not open. But it did have a rumble seat. Jim and I both thought $75 was a good deal. I believe I sold that car for $50 a year later when we moved to Chicago.

(O Perfect Love)

The Chicago Experience

I rob banks for a living. What do you do?
—John Dillinger

AT THE END OF SUMMER in 1951 Ruthie and I left a few things with sister Peg and Dale Swenson on their farm near Olds, Iowa, and set out to discover what life was like on a different campus in a big city. The seminary, one of the larger of the ten Presbyterian seminaries in the U.S., had been in Chicago since 1859, and in 1884 was renamed in honor of Cyrus McCormick, the industrialist. McCormick Seminary was in the Lincoln Park area on the north side of the city. The campus was large, with green trees and several buildings of impressive architecture, all surrounded by a tall corrugated black iron fence with occasional entry gates.

I was pleased to be accepted at McCormick, and I looked forward to my studies there. At the same time, I was anxious about the challenges of the program, my capacity to develop necessary abilities, and the certainty I would need for effective ministry. In other words, I thought more and more seriously about what a pastor really needs to do and who a pastor needs to be. Nevertheless, I had a strong desire to proceed with my plans.

We moved into a two-room apartment on campus, with our meals provided in a common dining area. Ruthie proceeded almost immediately to find a job in a bank across the street from the campus near the three-way busy intersection of North Halsted, North Lincoln, and West Fullerton streets. I was enrolled in the seminary's three-year Master of Divinity degree program. My Fall 1951 studies included New Testament and Old Testament exegesis courses, introductory courses in Hebrew and Greek Language, and a study of themes and traditions in Christian History.

As the semester progressed my course work was going well, Ruthie was in constant support of our plans, and our economic status was tolerable. Nevertheless, my anxieties grew. I had naively anticipated that one aspect of study at the seminary would be an immediate clarification, perhaps confrontation, concerning the "beyond experience" and miraculous events that pervade the scriptures and are held sacred and required by Christian dogma and participation. In my first semester classroom study of both Old and New Testament scriptures my impatience for clarifying, analyzing, explaining, or struggling with such basic beliefs overtook my judgement and contributed to my anxiety over my becoming an effective pastor. At the end of the semester I took stock of my mindset and concluded that I would not continue my studies at McCormick. After a time, I recognized that I should have been more patient, or more committed, but the decision was made.

Perhaps the urban context of the seminary contributed to the decision, although that is probably more excuse than reason. Growing up in the Council Bluffs-Omaha complex with little experience with cornfields and cows I had always thought of myself as a "city boy". The move to urban Chicago placed us in an exciting but completely foreign environment and challenged my understanding of living in a city. Soon after Ruthie began her bank job, she came home anxious to share an unnerving experience at the bank where she worked. Evidently the guards there had an additional duty of helping other bank employees with tasks such as obtaining supplies. In need of some envelopes, she had approached a guard from the rear, tapping on his shoulder. She said he whipped around, with his gun coming from his holster, giving Ruthie quite a fright.

Ruthie said the guard apologized and advised her, "Don't ever do that again."

There were other aspects of the neighborhood. Transportation to more pleasant shopping sites was by the "EL", the Chicago elevated train system with a station a couple of blocks from campus and requiring a knowledge of schedules and routes. A few steps down North Lincoln Street from the campus was the Biograph Theater, where famous mob member John Dillinger was shot by police in 1934.

The theater is still operating, and offers tours concerning Dillinger and the mob years of Chicago. In fact, several tours available in the area include the *Chicago Crime and Mob Tour*, the *Chicago Night Crimes Tour*, *Chicago's Original Gangster and Prohibition Tour*, and the *Private Al Capone Gangster Tour* – today the fee for that one is $660 each. That history seemed to add a negative tone to the neighborhood, whether real or imagined. The area surrounding the campus was an urban area facing problems of transition such as heavy traffic, an increasing rate of crime, evidence of poverty, and unkempt public areas.

A few years after we left McCormick the Board of Directors noted that the seminary's urban location "placed it in the swirling center of American societal conflict and change", citing several negative events impacting the seminary. In 1975 the McCormick campus relocated to the Hyde Park area of south Chicago near the University of Chicago and near a few other theological schools. The old McCormick property was acquired by DePaul University. It seems the concerns I felt about the "inner city" aspects of the McCormick campus came to be recognized as a significant factor by others.

I left McCormick but I had no intent to leave the church, and I remained committed to church membership and activity.

Eventually I became a Ruling Elder in the Presbyterian Church and served on the Session, or ruling body, and in other roles in the churches where I had membership. I served on committees in the North Central and East Iowa Presbyteries, and on committees of the Synod of Lakes and Prairies. Ruth also became a Ruling Elder and Deacon in the church and active in women's associations and church committees, making special contributions in the area of adult education.

High School Teaching

When one teaches, two learn.
> — Robert Heinlein

NOW, WHAT SHOULD I DO? With my career plans in doubt, I needed to scramble to set a new direction. Ruthie had been working constantly to keep us afloat, and I needed to move toward a new career choice. The logical choice was to begin teaching, but I could not proceed without some additional course work to meet certification requirements. My record of studies in language and literature as a teaching area was strong, but I needed to complete additional requirements in teaching methods and supervised teaching experiences.

I completed those requirements at the University of Iowa, with helpful guidance toward selecting courses that also provided graduate credit. I received a scholarship for these studies from the Wall Street Journal which came with the responsibility that I complete a course in Journalism.

I completed the teaching requirements during the summer of 1953 when two dramatic events occurred simultaneously. Early in the morning of July 4 a tornado struck Iowa City, toppling trees, and causing buildings to sway, including the top floor of Mercy Hospital where Ruthie was giving birth to Kent O'Dean Ratekin. We had fun relating Kent to tornadic conditions throughout his life, but that was unfair. He may have disturbed the peace of expected settings, but there were always good plans and good outcomes in his adventures. In August we packed everything we owned and baby Kent into our car and headed for Harlan, Iowa to fill my first teaching position. I was surprised to find that I was assigned to teach history as well as English courses, but I was pleased to be employed. Ruthie was also employed full time as a Business Education teacher. (We had arranged a safe setting for Kent.) I received $100 a month more than Ruthie received because I was head of family. That was a laugh. It was a productive year for my own development, if not for my senior history students.

An offer to teach in Oelwein, Iowa surprised and pleased us, placing us back to eastern Iowa and closer to Ruthie's family. I taught not only English but also journalism, taking advantage of my high school and college courses in journalism. The Journalism assignment included producing a two-page student newspaper which was published weekly in the Saturday tabloid of the local newspaper, the Oelwein Daily Register. At that time, the Oelwein newspaper used hot lead letterpress machines for the printing process. I was always amazed at the ability of typesetters to read copy upside down and backwards. I learned much about the production of a daily newspaper which was useful for my teaching. That contact lead to the Register's assigning me to write coverage of sporting events when they had no staff available – providing a useful additional bit of income. I was delighted with the efforts of the journalism students and they were pleased also when we received word that our publication had been awarded a top division 1 rating by the National Scholastic Press Association.

Ruthie was active in creating our own properly furnished two-story home, contributing to church and community activities, and caring for Kent, not a task for the idle. As a two-year-old Kent preferred to go up the stairway on the smidgen of step outside the railing and enjoyed removing every pan in the lower kitchen cabinets. On one occasion Kent was eating breakfast in his high chair near the window. Ruthie left the kitchen on a brief errand and the phone rang. Our neighbor said

Kent was OK. She had seen him crawl out the window, drop to the ground, and he was playing in the yard. Kent never lost his sense of adventure.

A WELCOME INVITATION

Horace (Herb) Hoover, principal of Oelwein High School, and his wife Joyce became good friends during our stay in Oelwein. Late in the spring of 1956 Herb announced that he was leaving Oelwein for a position at Dubuque Senior High School in Dubuque, Iowa. I was sad to hear he was leaving, but then he asked me if I was interested in going to Dubuque with him.

He explained that Dubuque Senior High wanted to start a special sophomore class in English for students with reading and writing needs. Evidently Herb had shared with the Dubuque Superintendent information about my efforts in one of my Sophomore English classes. I jumped at the chance to apply, Ruthie agreed, the application was approved, and in the fall of 1956, we found ourselves in a Dubuque apartment, near Senior High School, with Kent now three years old.

My responsibilities at Dubuque included teaching literature and language studies, a special language development class for sophomores, a journalism class, supervising the publication of a weekly student newspaper, and selling apples and candy bars at athletic events. After securing good homecare for Kent, Ruthie also joined the faculty at Dubuque Senior High, teaching courses in keyboarding and bookkeeping.

Ruthie volunteered for the additional responsibility of teaching a released time class in religion, an unusual offering for a public-school district. At the time, the religious affiliation of well over 60 percent of the population of Dubuque was Catholic, presenting a complex challenge in the distribution of financial support for education in the district. An original agreement had provided that Catholic students attending public schools would have released time for religious education. The evacuation from classrooms of such a large percentage of students created a problem for scheduling educational offerings. Finally, the district agreed to provide released time for religious study for both Catholic and non-Catholic students. Ruthie taught one of the released time classes in a protestant church.

The six years we lived in Dubuque, 1956 to 1962, formed a significant period of our lives. The city itself is delightful with its heritage, its vistas of the Mississippi valley, its architectural variety, and its institutions. We made many life-long friends there, and it was in Dubuque that we completed our family. Jack Grason was born during a snow storm on the Ides of March in 1957, and Joel Carlson was born on May 26, 1961, a beautiful spring day.

In 1959 we purchased our first new house, a classic starter three-bedroom ranch. To make it affordable, I agreed to do all the inside and outside painting and finishing the lawn with sod. When the sod came, I was enjoying classes in Iowa City. Ruthie was home outside laying sod and herding two kids when friend Herb Hoover drove by, saw her predicament, and stopped to help. Herb was a real friend. The good news was that my Iowa City studies allowed me to receive an M.A. degree at the end of summer 1959 and made possible a jump up the pay scale.

THE IMPOSSIBLE POSSIBILITY

Jesus answered, "I am the way and the truth and the life. No one comes to the father except through me." - John 14:6,

One event during our six-year stay in Dubuque has a special significance. We were part of a small social group of couples who originally gathered to party and play bridge. The group of 12 included an attorney, a musician, an obstetrician, a head basketball coach, a seminary professor, a couple of school teachers, and spouses. Enjoying our discussions as much as the bridge game, we asked Arthur Cochrane, one of our group and Professor of theology at the University of Dubuque Seminary, to start us on some kind of significant study. Arthur and his wife Ilsa agreed and suggested that we study *The Knowledge of God and the Service of God*, an analysis of the Scottish Confession by the Swiss theologian Karl Barth. Arthur was known to be a friend, translator, and advocate of Karl Barth. Under Arthur's patient guidance, and through much debate and argument, we became aware of meanings and problems of many Christian concepts and also Barth's concerns with some current directions of Christian thought.

Imagine our surprise in 1962 when Arthur Cochrane told us at one of our "social" meetings that Karl Barth was coming to the U.S.A., that he would be visiting Arthur concerning some of their mutual work, and that Barth was willing to meet with our small group. We discovered that the reason Barth was coming to the U.S. was to deliver a series of lectures at Princeton Theological Seminary in New Jersey, at Union Theological Seminary in New York, at the University of Chicago, and at San Francisco Theological Seminary. At that time Barth was a world-known theologian and author and had appeared on the cover of Time magazine. The fact that he also agreed to meet with 12 people in Dubuque, Iowa was unbelievable!

When Dr. Barth met with us, he began by saying, "What are your questions?" We were all quiet. What an opportunity! What a challenge! Finally, Mel Moeller spoke up. "I have a question. When Jesus told the disciples that they already knew the way to the Father, Thomas replied, 'How do I know the way?' and

Jesus said, 'I am the way.' That seems to mean that all persons who have not had a chance to meet or learn about Jesus, through no fault of their own, cannot be 'saved'."

And then she asked ""Is that true?"

Barth responded immediately, "That is an impossible possibility." He proceeded to explain that no person is outside the grace of God. His comments centered on the person of Jesus and the presence of God's spirit in Jesus, the presence of constant love revealed to Thomas through Jesus that defines the 'way' of God's love, a 'way' we all can express through our love toward others.

College Teaching

Old professors never die, they just lose their faculties.

— Stephen Fry

D URING THE YEARS WE WERE in Dubuque, our Alma Mater Parsons College in Fairfield had restructured its B.A. programs under new president Millard Roberts. That program included a year-round trimester system, and a three- tiered instructional program of large group lecture, small group interactions and individual tutoring sessions.

The underlying view was that many students entering college were overwhelmed by the amount of responsibility that faced them and often were unprepared for the disciplined study routines required for success, leading to their dropping out and not realizing their own capabilities. Parsons became known for its "second chance" opportunity for students to succeed in college.

PARSONS – A BRIDGE TO TENURE

Attracted to the possibility of teaching at the college level, I applied to Parsons, emphasizing my experiences in helping students in learning processes. I was accepted for a position in its English department and began teaching there in 1962. Ruthie also became employed at Parsons to work with students in the three-tiered program as a tutor in economics. I taught English Composition courses and a course in Reading and Study Skills for College Students. In Parsons' trimester program faculty taught for two semesters and pursued individual research and writing projects in one semester. This format allowed me to continue graduate work toward a doctorate degree at the

University of Iowa during semesters of the regular school year as well as teach full academic semesters at Parsons.

President Roberts had invested heavily in the recruiting program to attract "second-chance" students from wealthy families in the east, and the effort was notably successful. Ruth liked to share a tutoring experience with one of her students who was not interested in studying for a test. She explained the value of a degree for his future employment. He responded that he didn't need to worry about that because his dad owned a large national rifle manufacturing company. She suggested that his dad should come to take the test. I remember standing at a driveway waiting for several Corvettes to pass, driven by members of the campus "Corvette Club".

A COFFEE STOP IN SOLON

In 1962 after two years at Parsons we decided to return to the University of Iowa so that I could complete my studies in educational psychology. We had enjoyed being back with family and old friends in Fairfield. Kent and Jack were getting settled with school and friends, and Joel was up on two legs and running, so it was a bit difficult to leave Fairfield again. Nevertheless, Ruthie agreed, and we began looking for housing. We found a house in Solon, half-way between classes in Iowa City and Cornell college in Mt. Vernon where I was to teach a course in psychology. The outside of the house was attractive, newly painted with a new foundation. Inside we found a structure built no later than the 1920's, with wood flooring and woodwork in need of renewal. We found that the house had been moved from an area along the Iowa river which had been flooded to form the new Iowa City reservoir. But it fit our purposes. Ruthie claimed later that when she swept the kitchen floor, she didn't need a dustpan. All the "dust" had already fallen between the cracks in the flooring.

During the year we were in Solon I completed my course work, taught a class in psychology at Cornell, completed the research and writing for my doctoral dissertation, and worked for Reschly, the painting contractor. I regret that I spent little time with the boys during that period. Only years later did I hear about episodes of school events and trips to Lake McBride that Kent and Jack managed by themselves. I remember Ruthie telling me that Joel liked to go down the basement to watch the mice.

Mom and Dad came from Council Bluffs to attend the summer 1965 commencement ceremony when I received a Ph.D. degree in Educational Psychology from the University of Iowa. One evening Dad asked me what my dissertation was about. I jokingly told him I had already completed my oral exams, but he continued just like a committee member. I explained that my studies combined the areas of language and psychology into a field known as psycholinguistics, the mental processes of gaining meaning from language, in my case from written language or text. I shared what I discovered in my research, titled A Comparison of Language Structures in Three Fields of Writing. I was pleased that he was interested.

ISTC, SCI, AND UNI

In the summer in 1965 I assumed a position in the Department of Education and Psychology at The State College of Iowa (SCI) in Cedar falls. Previously named Iowa State Teachers College, the name had been changed to SCI in 1961and later in 1968 was changed again to The University of Northern Iowa. The Department also was reorganized, forming the Department of Curriculum and Instruction in which I became

Coordinator of the Reading and Language Arts program, taught undergraduate and graduate courses, and advised students in their undergraduate and graduate degree programs.

I survived student evaluations, met an expected flow of regular publications in juried journals and presentations at professional conferences, successfully applied for financial grants, and over the years moved through the promotion ranks to full professor.

As with most faculty, I was involved with professional activities as well as teaching, advising and publication. I was especially pleased and proud to be part of creating and serving as president of the Iowa Reading Association, an affiliate member of the International Reading Association. I also formed and served as adviser to the first, or Alpha, chapter of Alpha Upsilon Alpha, an academic honor society created under the International Reading Association. The honor society recognized excellence in the performance of students in reading and language arts programs at the undergraduate and graduate levels. There are now over 40 chapters of the Society in American Universities. Also, I was pleased to be invited to provide presentations at an international conference of the World Congress of Reading in Dublin, Ireland in 1982 and at the International conference of the International Reading Association in Stockholm, Sweden in 1990.

Ruthie completed her M.A. in Business Education from UNI in 1975 and carried out an impressive career teaching business and office education courses in Wayland, Oelwein, Dubuque, and Cedar Falls High Schools, and serving as a guest instructor in courses at the University of Northern Iowa Department of Business Education. She introduced the use of computers in the Cedar Falls High School Business Education Department, and often provided presentations at business education meetings and conferences. She sucessively became elected to Boards and officer positions in the Iowa Business Education Association, the North Central Business Education Association, and the National Business Education Association. Ruthie received the Distinguished Service Award from the Iowa Business Education Association in 1987 and the Lloyd C. Douglas Alumni Award from the University of Northern Iowa in 1989.

In addition to our working tasks, Ruthie and I enjoyed participating in a variety of community organizations. Some of Ruthie's community activities included serving as an Elder and Deacon in the Presbyterian Church, a member of the Victorian House Committee in the Cedar Falls historical Society, and president of chapters of the PEO Society Beyond her professional and community activities, Ruthie was a homemaker and a parent par excellence. She enjoyed entertaining and kept us all creatively cared for. When one of the boys would cause a bit of trouble for a neighbor, like a broken window, Ruthie would march with them to the neighbor to oversee apologies and restitution. I admired her for that.

I served as an Elder and Deacon in the Presbyterian Church and over the years served as an officer and board member of the Cedar Falls Rough Risers Kiwanis Club and served on the Executive Board of the Cedar Falls Historical Society.

Occasionally Ruthie and I would attend each other's professional meetings. I recall Ruthie joined me at an IRA National Convention in Miami, Florida. When the convention was over, we decided to drive to Key West, a four-hour drive through the keys and over 1,000 bridges (actually 42), to join the tourists looking for Hemingway. We wanted to see the house where he wrote much of *Farewell to Arms,* and, of course, sit on a bar stool where we could experience his ghost and a scotch and water.

Also, I remember joining Ruthie on a trip to Boston where she was attending a Board meeting of the National Business Education Association. We walked the Freedom Trail, explored Faneuil Hall, and were educated in the true story of Paul Revere's ride. I believe that was our only trip to Boston, and it was good to gain a mental image of Boston Common and the Old North Church.

The University and Cedar Falls were particularly good to us, and despite an occasional temptation to move, we remained there until we retired. Ruthie retired from teaching in the Cedar Falls Schools in 1990, with a barrage of plaques and presentations recognizing her teaching and professional contributions. There is no relation between Ruthie's retirement and the fact that I experienced a heart attack later that year resulting in a simple angioplasty treatment and a few days of hospital recovery. I returned to carry out some North Central Association Evaluation projects in the UNI Dean of Education's office, and then returned to teaching.

I retired in 1992, with a send-off party by the department. Marvin Heller, Coordinator of Elementary Education, and good friend of many years, had established the department's practice of honoring retirees with a classic arm chair, emblazoned with an official UNI coat-of-arms and a brass plate identifying the honoree. My chair had not yet arrived. Typical of Marv's concern and skill, at the retirement party he presented to me a small, crafted replica of the chair, produced in his own workshop, and signed by faculty members of the department. My intended chair soon arrived, but I value that tiny chair with all the signatures with special gratitude and memories.

Our Three Sons

If my son is happy, then I am happy!
—Chris Paul

RUTHIE AND I ENJOYED OUR three sons. There is a nine-year range from Joel through Kent, with Jack exactly in the middle. There were times through the years when successively each child was too young for a planned travel and was farmed out to Grandma and Grandpa or Aunt Peg and Uncle Dale, or they were too old with their own employment or schooling schedule and were left on their own to come home to an empty house. With abandonment as a child, and unmonitored freedom as a teenager, problems or snags were bound to occur. Yet they all survived as solid citizens, and I admire them for that.

On February 9, 1964, 11-year-old son Kent was watching the Ed Sullivan Show when the Beatles appeared, ending the evening with "I Want to Hold Your Hand". So began his dream of playing the guitar. We eventually recognized the depth of his desire and with advice found a proper Kay guitar and secured a local retired musician to teach Kent the basics. There are two parts to learning to play music: learning the music and learning the instrument. Kent tried hard—it's difficult to play a Kay guitar anyway—with results indicating the need for a change. The answer was an older teen-ager, Marty Bock, who had sidestepped the violin of his accomplished father Emil and was willing to share his guitar talent with Kent. Kent blossomed, playing for us, then friends, then on demand for entertainment and performances. His guitar became an expected traveler with him to family reunions and a professional tool with his classroom students studying language, history, music, and the dramatic arts. I have been impressed with his more recent development in classic guitar.

Kent was the best basketball player in Iowa, but the bias favoring height often left him on the bench. Nevertheless, he had many friends, maintaining friendships even to the present. He began working early, as if it was expected of him, mowing grass, staffing McDonalds, pumping gas, even eventually working as a computer attendant at Viking Pump in Cedar Falls while completing his B.A. in Art Education at UNI. Kent is a talented artist. For many years we enjoyed a mural painted on the wall of his room, and we have a valued collection of his Christmas card art. Kent has a strong commitment to the principles of Waldorf Education. He completed an M.A. in Education from the University of Detroit Mercy, became a founder and principal of the Whatcom Hills Waldorf School in Bellingham, Washington, taught in the Langley, Washington public schools and became principal of Waldorf schools in Oregon and California.

Always a seeker and a philosopher, Kent found the theosophy of Rudolph Steiner meaningful for understanding the needs and development of the children he teaches, a framework for his own life, and an understanding that often makes him a welcome counselor for others. In fact, Kent would serve as a useful model of someone who avoids bias of any type, by racial features, belief systems, body type, manner of dress, hair style, or any such basis for assumptions. Of course, he is always willing to share his views on a meaningful life.

Kent's wife Tricia is a seasoned gardener and a care giver for elderly adults. Kent acquired a Kubota garden tractor, and for some time together they created an extensive produce farm on their Whidbey Island property. One of their challenges was to keep the deer from eating their produce and eagles from stealing their chickens. Kent is retired but still active, serving as Faculty Liaison for Woodhaven High School, a Waldorf School under development in the South Whidbey Island school district on Whidbey Island, Washington. And, as always, he saves time to spoil his grandchildren Evelyn and Emily, children of daughter Shonee and Mike Hightower. Shonee has a position as a pharmaceutical archivist, and Mike is a Chief Petty Officer in the U.S. Coastguard.

Jack was the best football player at Valley Park Junior High School, but he quit the team, telling me "That's war, and I don't like war." Jack would rather fight his battles with words, and he became exceptionally good at it. He joined and enjoyed the Cedar Falls High School Debate team and appeared regularly in productions of the Speech and Dramatics Department. Jack received a B.A. in English at the University of Northern Iowa, and an M.A. in Strategic Communications from the University of Iowa. He served several Iowa state agencies including the Iowa Lottery, the Department of Agriculture, and the Department of Economic Development. He became a project analyst for Principal Financial Group and Director of Development for the Lions Eye Bank. More recently Jack formed Ratekin Communications, a consulting service for small businesses, and served a family of banks to ensure common communication procedures for group members. Jack's wife Lori serves as a resource specialist in the health insurance industry and lovingly monitored Jack's developing achievements in culinary activity.

Jack was a Ruling Elder and Deacon of the Presbyterian Church and enjoyed leading group studies within the church program. Also, Jack was a handy resource. If someone at a family affair asked, "How does sunshine produce energy?" or "how many teeth does a cat have?", or "What's the difference between theism and deism?" the response would be, "Ask Jack." We lost Jack's wise support and his constant good humor when he succumbed to brain cancer in October 2018. Jack seemed to have a magnet drawing him to "be there" for others. At his funeral one of his friends told me that Jack's counseling had literally saved his life.

Joel was the friendliest kid on the block and never lost his touch; wherever he is in the world people will find a ready friend. Joel always found work for himself, providing pizza, serving retail customers, even managing a retail business. As he progressed through college, I began to see an intriguing pattern in his selection of studies. His work included terms like design, architecture, and technology. He was creating a career in what has become known as Workplace Strategies, the effort of businesses to design workspaces that meet the needs of workers in the context of maximum production for employers. Joel completed his B.A. in Interior Design at the University of Northern Iowa and began his climb through positions in this relatively new field, designing work spaces for American Express and Capital One. He continued his education at the University of North Carolina at Chapel Hill, receiving a Master of Business Administration in International Business. He founded and was chairman of Cornet Global's Workplace Community and created his company, Ratekin Consulting, to help businesses use workplace design, mobile technologies, and other strategies to create work environments. He has moved on to positions at Gresham Smith and Partners and TD Ameritrade. Joel and Angie have always participated in churches and service to their community, and their faith is evident in their lives.

Joel's work with major businesses and corporations frequently placed him in the context of business expansions and contractions, corporate buyouts, and changes in corporate leadership, creating both opportunity and risk. I have never known someone when faced with serious uncertainty for the future who has reflected such a firm belief and assurance of future care and blessings as Joel. Joel and Angie are in constant contact and care for their four bright and beautiful daughters and their families, Lindsay and Matt Graham with children Benjamin, Joel, and Annika in Indiana, Elizabeth and Weston Reeves with children Tyler and Natalie in Virginia, Stephanie Ratekin in Virginia, and Hannah and Nate Word in Colorado. Early in their marriage, Joel's wife Angie provided in-residence care for handicapped adults, operated a preschool, and is now a nurse for patients under hospice care. Over the years they often have opened their home to persons in need of a place to be. It would be no exaggeration to say that Joel and Angie literally have a "sanctuary" home.

When our family was young, our summer vacations often took the form of a cabin for a week on a lake in Minnesota or Wisconsin, at a resort with our own dock and a boat holding poles and tackle ready for an hour or two at the last place we caught a fish. Over time the boys progressed, baiting their own hook with live bait or lure, landing their own fish, driving the boat, and eventually going out "alone". The summer came when schooling, work, or private plans gave the boys their own schedules, and Ruthie and I were back to fishing alone.

Ruthie was an accomplished fisherperson. and we enjoyed fishing together, although I didn't enjoy the occasional fishhook in a finger. One day I caught myself securely, with no removal of the hook as hard as Ruthie tried. We drove to the doctor who just pushed the hook through, cut off the barb, and dressed the wound. I told him I didn't know how that hook got on the back of my thumb. He pointed at a chart of a body outline on the wall and explained that those red x's marked where he had removed fish hooks that season. There were red x's all over that body, from toes to scalp.

Kent and Tricia Ratekin   Jack and Lori Ratekin

Joel and Angie Ratekin

Hooked On Travel

*Travel and change of place impart new vigor
to the mind.*

—Seneca

JAMES MICHENER'S 1971 NOVEL *THE Drifters* is described
as "a poignant drama of six young runaways adrift in a
world they have created out of dreams, drugs, and dedication
to pleasure." The action is in the era of the Viet Nam War, and
much of the story unfolds in Torremolinos located in a strip
of Spain's southern coast known as the Costa del Sol. It is a
heartbreaking but sympathetic account of youth's search for
meaning in a world that often defeats dreams.

By 1974 *The Drifters* had become a popular book, generating
many reflective discussions and comments by literary critics.
That year the UNI alumni association released its tour guide,
highlighting a trip to the Costa del Sol, with accommodations in
Torremolinos. Our good friends Mary Nan and R.L. Aldridge
announced they were signing up and encouraged us to join
them. We had never traveled "across the water" before, but
maybe now was the time. We read *The Drifters*, hoped we
wouldn't become too tainted by life along the Costa del Sol,
and signed up.

We were undereducated for the trip. It was our first full
day in Spain, and it was already well past 12:00 noon. We sat
waiting for service in an empty restaurant. Finally, the server
appeared, tying on his apron, and saying "¿Qué te gustaría?"
We looked at each other, looked at the menu and decided on the
meal of the day. He served what was obviously the appetizer.
We ate it all, and he brought another plate of food. We ate it
all, and he brought another plate of food. We were no longer

hungry. We learned that my Spanish was not sufficient, that the Meal of the Day was a several-course meal, and that the typical time for lunch is 2:00 or after.

We thoroughly enjoyed the adventure in Spain and confronted no Michener characters in trouble. We had a car and drove to a bull fight in Marbella and visited the Alhambra Palace in Granada. I remember on a Saturday seeing a group of workmen at the end of their work day sitting in a circle on the sidewalk sharing bread and Sangria and hearty laughs. It was a happy sight. We joined a trip across the Mediterranean past the monkeys on Gibraltar to the Kasbah in Tangier, Morocco in north Africa. After that trip to Spain, we knew there would be more travel. In the 26 years between 1974 and 2000 we enjoyed 15 international trips to 26 different nations, most of them European, and often with repeated visits to the same countries. Our most frequent repeated visits were the four we took to Sweden to visit families related to Ruthie's heritage.

A VISIT TO THE HOMELAND

In 1982 I gave a presentation at a meeting of the World Congress of Reading in Dublin, Ireland. I thought a visit to Mom's roots in England and Dad's heritage in Ireland would interest them both. With a couple of overseas trips, one to England, under our belts, Ruthie and I thought we could design a tour that would be comfortable for my 80-year-old parents. In the end we should have been more concerned about our own endurance. Mom's list included Westminster Abbey, Buckingham Palace, Stonehenge, a trip through the Cotswold villages, and tea and scones. Dad was willing to see a real Irish pub, and to find out what kissing the Blarney stone was all about.

We arrived in London, spent two days touring several London sights and had tea at The Rose Lounge near Piccadilly Circus. We took the hour flight to Dublin, rented a car, checked-in at the Egan's B & B, and then had dinner at The Maples nearby. After dinner Mom and Dad walked to the B&B while Ruthie and I strolled around the block. When we returned, we found Mom quite upset. Dad explained that while they were standing in front of our lodging, a motorcycle with two men stopped, one of the men ran over and pulled Mom's purse from her arm, and they sped away. The hostess at Egan's helped us notify the police, or Garda, to report the theft.

The next morning the Garda called, they had found the purse in a trash container in downtown Dublin, and they would come by to take us to the police station to identify the purse. Mom was happy. Her money was gone, but all else, including passport, medicine, tickets, and other things that go in a purse were still there. The two friendly Garda (short term for Guardian of the People) who drove us back to Egan's wanted to know all about the United States. One indicating a desire to visit San Francisco.

The World Congress meetings were in Dublin Castle, a site of government in Ireland since the year 1204. Charles Dickens preceded me there as a speaker in 1864. In contrast to Dickens, my remarks were never widely published. After I had completed my conference duties, Dad recalled that he had an uncle who once lived in Cork in southern Ireland and asked if we could drive there to see the city. At dinner after we arrived in Cork, a server suggested we might want to attend an event scheduled that evening in a school gymnasium. We looked into it, and there we found an authentic, real, honest to goodness Irish Ceilidh in progress - a performance of Gaelic folk music with singing, dancing, much fiddle, and storytelling presented by volunteers with little pause between events. It was very much worth the trip to Cork.

When we returned to England from Ireland, we did more touring, which included watching the pageant of the Changing of the Guard at Buckingham Palace. We also decided to do some celebrity searching. Standing on the sidewalk outside St. Paul's Cathedral we saw Queen Elizabeth, Prince Charles and Diana, and Prime Minister Margaret Thatcher arriving for the Falklands Reconciliation Service, an attempt to show good will to Argentina following the end of that strange war.

The Garda watch Mom check the
contents of her purloined purse.

THE GRAND TOUR

We frequently traveled with Dr. James and Mary Ann Schnur. Jim was my Department Head at UNI, moving on to the position of Dean of Education at Lamar University in Texas and then Dean of Education at the University of Southern Mississippi. Mary Ann was a special educator, teaching students in communities where they lived. We maintained our friendship over the years through occasional visits and international trips together, including travels to England, France, and Austria. Friend Peter Leuthold who served as a hospital administrator in the US Air Force invited the four of us, together with friends Phyllis McGowan, Vine Baiotto, and Jackie Leuthold, to visit him at his current station in Izmir, Turkey.

On June 20, 1983, we came together in Izmir where Peter had arranged for us to room in a large apartment. Water is rationed in Izmir, and Peter explained that the swimming pool at our complex was a bit misleading because it was filled only once a season, with no filtering or changes of water. Also, he explained, the water in our building was shut off at 10:00 at night, and not turned on until morning. He suggested that we take care of bath and toilet needs before that time, and then he distributed several empty five gallon buckets with the orders to go to the swimming pool, fill our buckets, and have them ready to use for supply to the toilets for any use during the night. It was just enough cultural difference to make the experience interesting and laughable rather than a chore.

Over the next few days Peter directed a fascinating tour of local areas in Turkey. We traveled to the ancient coliseum in Ephesus and stood on the spot where Paul delivered his speech to the Ephesians. We visited the bazaars of Izmir where some of our group bought valued hand-spun wool and silk Izmir carpets to be shipped home. We stayed for a night at a beach hotel in the resort community of Kusadasi on the Aegean coast, and to top it off, we swam in the Aegean Sea, personally meaningful to me due to the sea's association with Greek mythology and the neo-classic character Lord Byron who was a strong swimmer.

Our trip to Turkey was over too soon, but there was more to come. We flew from Istanbul to Rome and filled two days visiting the ancient Roman sites - the Forum, the Colosseum, the Parthenon, Trevi Fountain, and the Vatican, a surreal experience for me. We stood in St. Peter's Square, saw Pope John Paul II appear in his window, and waited for his greeting in English.

The eight of us traveled in a large van, driving north from Rome with the goal of eventually reaching Zurich, Switzerland to catch our flight home. Along the way we visited the hill towns of Orvieto, and Siena, stopped at Pisa where Ruthie wanted to go higher up the Leaning Tower than I did, stayed overnight in Florence to visit art galleries and Michelangelo's David, and viewed Leonardo da Vinci's Last Supper, still under restoration, in Milan. Our route took us past Lake Como, which gets my vote for the most beautiful lake in the world, and we finally reached the alps. No one was anxious to drive in the alps. Peter, originally a native of Switzerland, finally agreed to take the wheel to drive the curvy alpine highways with few guard rails.

Now in Switzerland, we drove to Zermatt and took a train up the mountainside to lodging where there was a splendid view of the Matterhorn. We had a rare view of the mountain peak in the moonlight undisturbed by clouds. I couldn't help but think of my fifth-grade social studies book that had pictures of the Matterhorn and English soldiers in their tall black hats guarding the king. Now I had seen both, except the soldiers I saw were guarding the Queen, not the King.

VISITING FAMILY IN SWEDEN

In 1990 I was scheduled to provide a presentation at a conference of the International Reading Association in Stockholm, Sweden. We decided that would be a good time for Ruthie to continue to explore some of her family relations there. We were accompanied by Cedar Falls friends Bob and Jean Hall. Bob had long desired to locate and visit his ancestral home in Sweden, and we invited them to travel with us.

With the aid of the Swenson Swedish Immigration Research Center at Augustana College in Rock Island, Illinois, we found names of current relatives of Ruthie's parents Fred and Minnie in Sweden. The English-speaking volunteer in Sweden who located the relatives provided addresses and agreed to be a translator for us when we arrived.

It was an exciting experience as we drove up the farm lane, past Swedish cows, and were welcomed into the farm home of Janne and Ingrid Östberg and adult son Lasse in Brismene near Falköping, Sweden. Janne and Lasse could speak a bit of English. Anna-Lena Hultman who had helped us locate the family drove the 20 miles from her home in Hösna and was extremely helpful in our getting acquainted. Lasse, the Sexton of their local church, gave us a tour of the church he maintains, showing us their ancient baptismal font, and their unbelievably tidy and picturesque graveyard, a characteristic of Swedish churches.

We also met Lennarth Frannson, a cousin in his 60's who lives in Falköping, and his sister Birgit who lives in their old family farm home near Brismene. We discovered that Lennarth, in addition to his native Swedish, was quite competent in English and in six other languages. Lennarth, now retired, was an engineer who needed to communicate personally with colleagues in several different countries in Europe. "Swedish is too small," he explained when we asked about his fluency.

During a visit to Lennarth's home he needed to take a quick trip to a drugstore. He entered his garage and came out on a bicycle. In Sweden it seems that a car is not necessary for short trips, no matter your age. One evening Lennarth drove us to the home of a friend who had invited all of us to dinner. Before dinner, the host served a generous glass of wine to all of us except Lennarth. Then he brought Lennarth a thimble of wine. We all laughed at the reminder that Sweden has extremely strict laws concerning drinking and driving.

In searching for family in Sweden we kept in mind an interesting custom related to surnames. The word "son" in Swedish has the same meaning as in English. The custom was, for example, to give the son of Adam the surname Adamson, or the son of Jacob as Jacobson. The same was true of daughters, resulting in Adamsdotter, and Jacobsdotter. Ruthie's great grandfather in Sweden was named Peter Larsson, and his son, Ruthie's grandfather, was named Wilhelm Petersson. The extra "s" was often dropped in the surname, as was use of "dotter". We can pretty accurately guess that Ruthie's great grandfather's first name was Lars. When Wilhelm Petersson came to America, he decided to Anglicize his given name to William, and due to the confusing abundance of Petersons in the Swedish immigrant community, he decided to adopt the surname of an ancestral "town soldier", Odean. Evidently in Sweden's past someone who was not fond of his surname could just start using another one.

We had learned that the family we were visiting in Sweden was related to Ruthie's father, Frederick William O'Dean. Fred knew that when his father came to America in 1869, he changed his name from Wilhelm Edvard Peterson to William Edward

O'Dean. In discussion with Janne and Ingrid and son Lasse, we determined that Ingrid is descended from one of the sisters of Ruthie's grandfather, William O'Dean. Therefore Fred, Ruthie's father and Ingrid, Lasse's mother have the same grandparents.

We left Sweden and continued on the trip we had planned with Bob and Jean, which included a visit to East Berlin, recently opened to visitors, and a visit to Prague, Checkoslovakia, also recently available to international travelers. In Prague we found several memorials still prominent honoring local citizens' efforts in 1969 to "humanize" their Russian controlled government, an effort known as the Prague Spring. Also, on a tour we learned the origin of the term "defenestration" as a method of punishment, based on the settlement of a dispute by throwing a troublemaker out of a high window in the palace.

We continued our travel through East Germany to Berlin. East Germany had decided to remove the wall separating the East and West sections of Berlin in November 1989, and when we arrived there in July,1990 much of the concrete wall remained, but with many openings, many chips removed for souvenirs, and considerable graffiti. The economic differences between East and West Germany in building conditions, public facilities, and available goods in stores was astounding.

When we began traveling in Europe in the 1960's I was pleased to find that we could often communicate in English, or at least be referred to another person nearby who recognized our English. In fact, I probably had a larger problem communicating in English in Ireland and Wales than in some non-English speaking countries. With studies in Spanish, French, and German I still lacked the confidence to chat comfortably with native speakers. Obviously, I had learned to read but not converse in those languages.

THE TIME SHARE PHENOMENON

All significant events have their moment, and the moment that led us to our becoming time share owners came on a vacation when we decided to investigate a shopping mall instead of going fishing, dine in a friendly restaurant instead of cleaning and cooking fish, and relax with cable TV instead of adjusting rabbit ears. That's when we received the letter offering a free three-day vacation in an upscale resort condo with the only expense being to survive a short presentation on the joys of owning a time-share.

The three days in northern Minnesota were really one day with one day coming and one day leaving. The short presentation was more than three hours, a portion of which was spent as a captive in a van traveling to where we could examine one of the new condos we could own for one week of the year, sharing with the other 51 one-week owners of the same condo.

Finally, the third tier of the sales force offered a sacrificial price, we capitulated and became time-share owners. After 20 years of ownership, we never stayed during the specific week or at the condo we had purchased. An additional "time share exchange" program, at additional expense, allowed us to trade our week of ownership for other weeks at other resorts in the US and in many parts of the world. Usually traveling with friends or family, we enjoyed repeated stays in Minnesota, Oregon, Missouri, Colorado, Tennessee, and Iowa, and we enjoyed our foreign time-share stays in England, Ireland, France, Canada, and Mexico.

Then came the time when we realized that we would no longer be traveling and using our time-share ownership. Nevertheless, the real estate taxes and maintenance fee charges continued. It may be helpful to realize that responsibilities for overseeing the needs of time share properties are assumed by volunteer owners' committees of a time share property. The actual care, refurnishing, and upkeep of the time-share condos are carried out by management companies hired by these owners' committees. The management companies have no investment or other financial responsibilities for the condo communities. In other words, there is no entity to receive ownership from an owner wishing to return or stop ownership while the taxes and maintenance fees continue.

Out of this situation a new vocation was born separating timeshare owners from their timeshare obligations. For a price, there are now persons, businesses, that will remove an owner's legal obligation to pay taxes and fees, usually with little or no recovery or credit for the original investment. I engaged this assistance, and now I pay no taxes or maintenance fees on the time-share I purchased 35 years ago, although I still receive calls from persons offering to relieve me of my time share ownership, at a price.

We never regretted our participation in the time share program. We had a week's stay with Jim and Mary Ann Schnur and Vine Baiotto at Val d'Isere, France, site of events during the 1992 winter Olympics. We had lodging in the Cotswold villages in England with Ruthie's sister Peg and her husband Dale Swenson. We swam and flew a kite on the Oregon coast with Kent and his daughter Shonee when she was only 9 years old. We enjoyed a week in Canada with Mom and Dad and Ruthie's sister Lucille, and several weeks with each other in Minnesota and Wisconsin time-share facilities. We were satisfied with the return of our investment in the convenience and prepaid value of all the places we stayed under our timeshare arrangements.

Vine Baiotto

Dr. Jim and Mary Ann Schnur

Even the finest of travelers may say
"No more cathedrals will I see today."

—For Jim

THE

Carlson

HOUSE
A BED AND BREAKFAST

The World Of B&B's

Bed and Breakfast – We make both!
—Anonymous

A TIME-SHARE PROVIDES PLEASANT ACCOMMODATIONS IN an interesting setting, but it has an obvious limitation. It requires travel to the touristy area where a time share is available rather than providing lodging wherever travel is planned. There are always hotels, of course, but we have found that bed and breakfasts are generally available on any travel route for any length of stay with congenial hosts, a creative breakfast occasionally with other travelers, all at a reasonable rate. Therefore, our advance reservations often included B&B's.

We knew that some tolerance may be needed. At a B&B stop with my Mom and Dad in Stow-on-the-Wold in England the family cat "Emma" occasionally strolled into our room, sat, and watched us. Also, B&B proprietors can help. In Dover, a

B&B host asked us if there was anything we wanted to do while we were there. I happened to mention that I had never thrown darts in a pub. "I know just the place," he said and took us to a nearby pub for a great new experience throwing darts. Also, the variety can be interesting. At a B&B on a blueberry farm in Nova Scotia, our breakfast included blueberry pancakes with blueberry syrup, topped off with a blueberry coffee cake and a parting gift of blueberry jam.

From time to time Ruthie and I considered operating a B&B, often taking note as we traveled of aspects of the business to include or avoid. The condition that always saved us from actually doing such a thing was the challenge of locating a facility that already existed or that could be transformed into a proper setting for a B&B. Ruthie had already retired, and I was set for retirement within a few months when Ruthie received word that her Aunt Margaret Carlson, sister-in-law to Ruthie's mother, had died. Margaret was the latest occupant of a prominent Swedesburg, Iowa home built by an immigrant Swedish farmer when he retired to town in the early 1900's. Ruthie talked with her cousin Edward, Margaret's son living in New Mexico, arranged a time to view the property, and then we had a real problem.

The house, with a few improvements and alterations, was perfect. The residents of Swedesburg, proud of their Swedish heritage and of maintaining their population of 100 for 100 years, welcomed our intentions. Our problem was: Could a B&B survive in such a small town, with Mount Pleasant 10 miles to the to the south with several hotels, and Iowa City 40 miles to the north with abundant lodging?

The village was unincorporated, but surprisingly it does have a post office, and the Swedesburg community under the leadership of Louise Unkrich had just created the Swedish Heritage Museum in a building previously the town store, on the property next door to the Margaret Carlson house. Edward, who had been concerned about the fate and upkeep of the property, presented us with an attractive purchase price and we were happy to accept. In addition, Ruthie was a Swede and known by several residents in the area which no doubt helped our reception into the community.

The house is in the style known as American Foursquare, a symmetric shape with four large rooms on the main floor, four large rooms on the second floor, a finished attic with dormers on the sides, a central front doorway, a full width porch with a side wrap around, and a few small interior rooms. Inside on the left of the entrance hallway are a front parlor and a back parlor with sliding pocket doors available separating the rooms and entrance doors to the hallway. The dining room on the right is separated from the hall with cabinets and pillars. A doorway leads to the kitchen at the rear. The turn-back stairway to the second floor has a window landing, and at the top of the stairs a large central space with doorways to four bedrooms, a sewing room, a bath, and the stairway to the attic. There was even a clothes chute to the washing area in the basement.

The Reschly Construction Company in Olds, Iowa, a mile north of Swedesburg, bravely agreed to carry out renovations and additions that we requested. They completed a remarkable transformation of the home, often suggesting and providing improvements to our original amateur ideas and drawings. They revised the kitchen area, extending it into an area that was previously a porch and storage space, relocated the sink and cabinets with new windows above, and added an island and a tabled seating area. A bathroom was created on the main floor, the original second floor bath was updated, and baths were added for the second-floor bedrooms. A fireplace with flames from artificial fire logs, and a window were added to the back parlor. A deck was added along the dining room side of the house and extended beyond the house with an outdoor whirlpool jacuzzi, and electrical and telephone lines were updated as needed. Our total contractor's fees approached the amount of our original purchase price, but we were pleased with the results.

After we moved in, I converted the basement into an office, living, and sleeping areas, adding paneled walls, carpeting, and a ceiling with recessed lighting. Also, I added a roofed and screened area on a large section of the outside deck. That space became a popular serving area.

We refinished the light oak woodwork on the first floor, did some painting on the outside, and realized we needed a name and customers. We decided "The Carlson House" would reflect family connections and appeal to the local Swedish heritage. A sign company in nearby Lockridge created a permanent lawn sign with the name and traditional Swedish folk-art. We produced a brochure and distributed copies for travel stops and tourist agencies. Kent gave us a great gift with a drawing of the Carlson House that was included on the brochure, on calling cards, and with all of our advertising. I designed a website and joined listings by bed and breakfast organizations.

GRAND OPENING

Then Ruthie had a brilliant idea. Why not start by serving lunches or brunches for local groups as a way to get people in the house for a tour? We had already completed our state inspection for food service and posted our certificate, so the invitation went out to a few local groups to come to the Carlson House for lunch and a tour. We had an immediate response and discovered that word-of-mouth was a powerful means of advertising, receiving calls requesting lunch and a tour with that woman "who told jokes on a tour of the house". I never realized how many clubs exist in a community. From Mt. Pleasant, Winfield, Olds, Wayland, Crawfordsville, and other nearby towns we served birthday clubs, book clubs, day-of-the-week clubs, church clubs, art clubs, and others.

The Carlson House Bed and Breakfast opened for business in May 1993, offering a night's lodging and full breakfast for $45.00 and a group brunch at $6.00 each. Our B&B bookings grew, and so did interest in the brunches. Both menus had a Swedish influence, often offering Swedish pancakes with lingonberries and potatiskorv (Swedish sausage), Swedish oven-baked pancakes (ungspannkaka), and a brunch casserole. I usually was in the kitchen tending to the food preparation, while Ruthie had the joy of serving the tables and supervising additional help which we needed at times. I think I had more joy than Ruthie. The amount of our business allowed us to nudge up the prices a bit over the years. A convenient and enjoyable aspect of B&B ownership was that we had room to host many of our own family members for special occasions.

The B&B kept us busy, but we had ample time to enjoy community activities in Swedesburg and in Mount Pleasant. Our major attachment was to our neighbor the Swedish Heritage Society and to the Society's museum. We served on committees, served on its Board, and applied for and received annual grants to the museum from the Iowa Historical Resource Development Program, and special grants from other agencies including the Carver Foundation and the Kresge Foundation.

Both of us became active in the Presbyterian Church in Mount Pleasant, serving on local church and presbytery committees. The church's Mariners Club gave us many good times with social gatherings in member's homes, picnics in the park, and learning experiences. I became a member of the Iowa Foster Care Review

Board for Henry County, the Henry County Historical Society, and the Henry County Historic Preservation Board.

Ruthie became Treasurer of the Swedish Heritage Society, and a member and then President of the Southeast Iowa Symphony Orchestra Board. During the months of January and February we shuttered the B&B and joined snowbirds wintering on the Gulf of Mexico, first on Perdido Key near Pensacola, Florida and then in Orange Beach and Gulf Shores, Alabama. We came to feel at home on the Gulf and often hosted family and friends there.

CELEBRATIONS

Toward the end of 1999 anticipation of the turn of the century into the year 2000 created anxiety in the populace as well as plans for celebration. News reports reflected concern over how computers would respond to the new calendar and the possibility of some "marauding time spirits" creating havoc in general. The new century gave us a more important reason for concern and celebration – the 50th anniversary of our marriage on June 4, 1950. We made a reservation for the event at Dave and Carmen's Iris Restaurant, a popular event center for Mount Pleasant, and sent out invitations.

They all came, including my 98-year-old mother from Council Bluffs, my brothers with their families, Ruthie's near and distant relatives, many new local friends, old college friends, and close friends from Cedar Falls and UNI. Sons Kent, Jack, and Joel presented a humorous and nostalgic program of pictures from the past. Grand-daughter Libby sang, everybody took pictures of everybody else. Angie, Joel's wife, had prepared a photo album with artwork and comments that became a basic reference for us for years. We had a memorable celebration.

We enjoyed our ten-year stay in Swedesburg. We were close to Ruthie's sister Peg and daughter Linda and Tim Proctor in Mount Pleasant, and we often had dinner with brother Loren and Betty in Burlington. We met and enjoyed fascinating visitors including travelers from Sweden, visiting guests of Iowa Wesleyan University such as the Secretary of Agriculture from Lithuania, visiting family of Swedesburg and Mt. Pleasant residents, and a number of friends from Dubuque and Cedar Falls. Also, we gained a host of new friends. Our greatest regret during our time there was the death of Peg's husband Dale Swenson on the day in October,1992, that we moved into the Carlson House. Peg and Dale had come from Mount Pleasant to welcome us to Swedesburg and to help us in the moving process.

A NEW BEGINNING

We had realized a satisfying return on the B&B in both finances and experiences, but by 2002 we were getting a bit low on energy and we began looking forward to a return to symphony, football, and friends in Cedar Falls — in other words a real retirement. News came to us that a group from the University of Northern Iowa was planning a new retirement community designed for retirees from UNI located on a plot of land on Green Hill Road overlooking the campus, a location I had often admired. The Carlson House was placed on the market as a B&B, and we moved to an independent living facility in Mount Pleasant to wait for the sale and the development of the retirement community in Cedar Falls.

Fortunately, the Carlson House soon had a buyer who purchased it as a home not as a B&B. We received word that the UNI retirement project was abandoned, and we became thankful it was. The Western Home retirement facility in Cedar

Falls announced a new development of independent living retirement homes, known as Villas, on its south campus. In 2001 we chose the location of our future Villa on Iris Drive from an architect's map and waited for its construction. We moved in on December 2, 2002, well pleased with our new home and eager to integrate back into the fun and useful activities of retirement.

Moving is difficult. Our survival of several moves over ten years was made possible by the willing help of our sons and their wives. Kent and Tricia always have a plan, setting the order of progress, and making piles of stuff disappear, Joel and Angie helped not only packing but picking out what was worth moving, and Jack always kept humor in the process of moving by saying things like: "I found a bunch of kittens in a suitcase on the street and I immediately called the SPCA. They asked me: 'Are they moving?' I said, 'I'm not sure, but that would explain the suitcase.'"

Ruthie was pleased as punch to be back in Cedar Falls, rejoining the PEO chapter she helped establish over 30 years previously, helping to form a new Red Hat Club, playing bridge with old friends, and preparing devotions for the Church's Martha Circle. She tolerated the noise of football in the Dome, primarily enjoying the pre-game party of the Panther Scholarship Club. We again appreciated the creative performances of the Waterloo-Cedar Falls Symphony and rejoined the First Presbyterian church and the Cedar Falls Historical Society. I came back to the Rough Risers Kiwanis Club and, of course, we both enjoyed just being back among old friends.

Among those friends are Dr. Marvin and Sandra Heller. Over many years we have traveled with them to local and distant retreats, Road Scholar experiences, and explorations. Marvin, Coordinator of Elementary Education at UNI, and Sandra, Secretary of the Geography Department, are now both retired, although Marv has never really retired. As a member of the Kiwanis Rough Risers he has led many projects for community park and sports facilities, Hartman Reserve Nature Center, Habitat for Humanity, and projects of Nazareth Evangelical Lutheran Church. Marvin and Sandra had visited us often in Swedesburg and on the Gulf, they helped us get oriented to changes in an enhanced Cedar falls, and they supported us well through Ruthie's later difficulties.

Our last travel adventure abroad was a return to Sweden with a group of several friends from Swedesburg. The trip was planned for each traveler with special visits to the home areas from which their families had immigrated approximately 100 years previously. The visits were primarily made by stops at the beautiful Swedish cemeteries where the parents and siblings of those early migrants were buried. It was a moving sight to see the members of our party contemplating over the graves of their family members who had remained in Sweden. We extended that trip with travel through Norway, a beautiful land with vistas worthy of a final trip abroad.

Dr. Marvin and Sandra Heller

Troubling Times

Ever has it been
That Love knows not
Its own depth until
The moment of separation.

— *Kahlil Gibran*

W E CONTINUED ENJOYING CEDAR FALLS and wintering on the Gulf for about ten years when one day Ruthie came to me with a slip of paper, saying "This is a word I need to know when I go to PEO meetings. Keep it for me so when I go to the next meeting you can remind me what the word is." I was surprised because Ruthie always had a firm memory, much better than mine, and always ready with the grandchild's name that I couldn't remember.

Over a period of time I recognized that Ruthie's memory problem was increasing, so during an appointment with her medical doctor, Steve Erickson, we inquired about it. He gave her the classic short memory test and scheduled an additional evaluation at her next appointment. Dr. Erickson then explained to me that Ruthie was displaying increasing dementia, advised me on the sequence of probable future events, and scheduled appropriate professional appointments.

Ruthie refused to let her physical challenges interfere with enjoying our days back in Cedar Falls, agreeing with Kitty O'Neill Collins that "Aging seems to be the only available way to live a long life." Inherited arthritis led to aching hands, a knee replacement, and treatments for spinal stenosis. The effects of macular degeneration were stayed for a time under treatments at the University of Iowa Eye Care Clinic, but eventually left her with limited vision and surrender of her driver's license.

Starting in 2011 Ruthie began to experience occasional seizures, leaving her unconscious for a period of time and diagnosed as a TIA (Temporary Ischemic Attack). The first was in the air as we were landing in Minneapolis to connect with a flight to Seattle for a family get-together. With continued attacks, two or three a year, Ruthie came under the care of a neurologist who provided additional medications. By this time Ruthie had received several diagnoses, summarized in the general category of vascular dementia.

In 2015 we began a series of Western Home care programs. At Home with Western Home provided daily care for Ruthie in our Villa. What a great help our caregiver, Lindsey, was to us for almost a year, daily helping Ruthie prepare and dress for the day, fixing breakfast, checking Ruthie's vitals, helping with medications, and chatting with Ruthie and keeping her comfortable.

Early in 2016 Ruthie moved to the Western Home Martin Center, an assisted living facility providing 24-hour care, including skilled nursing, therapy facilities, and varied social activities. With increasing needs for assistance, Ruthie moved to the Western Home Nation Cottage, a surprising at-home facility for 15 residents designed as a family home with a comfortably furnished great room with a fireplace, an open kitchen, and spacious private bedrooms with bathroom and shower.

The professional nursing and supervisory staff in the Nation Cottage was excellent providing careful, thoughtful, and even entertaining services, constantly adjusting to Ruthie's special needs. Ruthie's movements were now limited to a wheel chair, with special equipment to move her in and out of bed. I was free to join Ruthie for all meals and daily joined Ruthie in the living area of the Cottage, often joining in the programs and activities provided and chatting with residents and other visiting spouses.

The supervising nurse and the cottage coordinator met with me frequently to help me understand Ruthie's current health and status. In November 2017 they advised me, and I agreed, to place Ruthie under hospice care.

During the night of December 30, 2017, the hospice staff informed me that Ruthie had died. I joined them at the cottage where they held a brief but meaningful service at her bedside. Funeral services were held at the First Presbyterian Church on January 5, 2018, and Ruthie was buried in the New Sweden Chapel cemetery in Jefferson County, Iowa, next to the church she attended as a child.

Ruthie and I shared a joyful and fulfilling life of adventure together for over 67 years. Her loss is great, but family, friends, and my church community have helped ease my grief, and I have many grateful memories of her love and wisdom at the heart of our family.

New Sweden Chapel
Jefferson County, Iowa

Reflections

O N November 8, 2018, my brother Jim put the final changes for his memoir, *It's Me: One Lucky Guy* on a thumb-drive and stuck it in his pocket. Jim lived in Paradise, California, a well-deserved location for his retirement years. That day the Camp Fire, the most destructive fire in California history, destroyed Paradise. The only remaining evidence of Jim's home after the fire was a stone bird bath. Previously Jim had lost his wife, and now he had lost his home, all the history that it contained, and any copies of his memoir.

With his memoir retained on his thumb-drive, he wrote an additional epilogue describing his harrowing escape, the uncertainty of his future, and explaining that he decided not to change the name of his work. He stated that with "my life, my health, a very supportive family, and many friends . . . I am still the luckiest guy in the world."

I admire Jim's outlook, and have come to understand that perhaps it is not wealth or status or achievements that make our lives "lucky". Rather it is the love and acceptance of family, friends, and strangers in spite of the faults and needs that make such acceptance seem impossible, the impossible possibility. If there are two luckiest guys in the world, I am the other one.

Printed in the United States
By Bookmasters